Fly Traps!

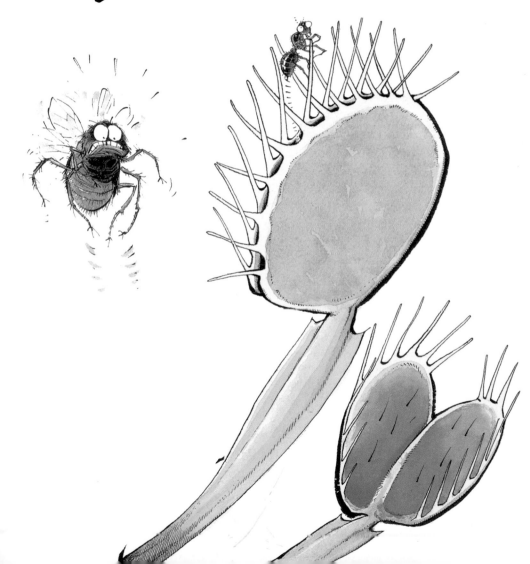

For Celia Daisy
M.J.

For Gary, Mary, Mark and Catherine –
The James Gang
D.P.

First published 1996 by Walker Books Ltd
87 Vauxhall Walk, London SE11 5HJ

This edition published 2010

2 4 6 8 10 9 7 5 3 1

Text © 1996 Martin Jenkins
Illustrations © 1996 David Parkins

The moral rights of the author and illustrator
have been asserted

This book has been typeset in Bembo Educational

Printed in China

British Library Cataloguing in Publication Data:
a catalogue record for this book is available from the British Library

ISBN 978-1-4063-1864-7

www.walker.co.uk

Fly Traps!

Plants that bite back

Martin Jenkins

illustrated by

David Parkins

WALKER BOOKS
AND SUBSIDIARIES
LONDON · BOSTON · SYDNEY · AUCKLAND

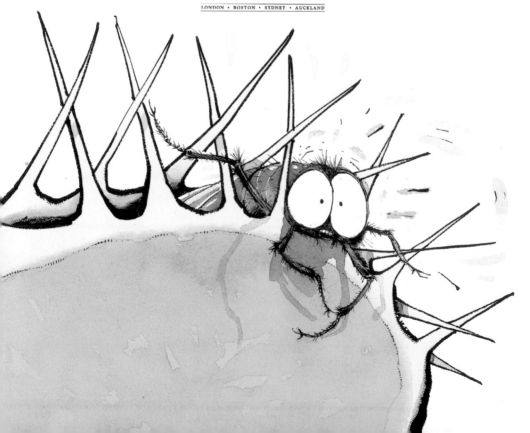

People do all sorts of things
in their spare time. There are
yogurt-pot collectors and people
who make models out of bottle
tops.

There are
beetle-spotters ...

and giant-leek growers.

Me, I like watching carnivorous plants. Carnivorous plants are plants that eat animals.

It all started
with a plant
I found in a
pond. It had
little yellow
flowers sticking
out of the
water.

Under the water there were tangled stems with hundreds of tiny bubbles on them. A friend told me it was called a bladderwort.

She said the bubbles on the stems were the bladders. Each one had a trapdoor shut tight, with little trigger hairs around it.

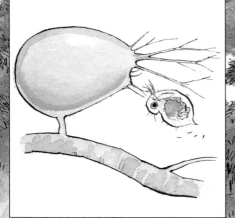

Whenever a water flea or other bug touched a hair, the trapdoor swung back and in the bug went.

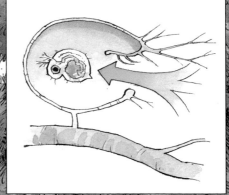

Then the trapdoor jammed shut and there was no way out. All in the twinkling of an eye.

Gosh, that's clever, I thought. The trouble was, the traps on my plant were so small that I couldn't really see them work. Well, I decided, I'll just have to find a bigger carnivorous plant.
So I did.

I had to climb a mountain, mark you,
and walk through all its
boggiest, mossiest places.
But there in the moss were little red
plants, shining in the sun. I thought
they were covered in dewdrops, but
they weren't. They were sundews, and
the shiny bits were sticky like honey.

I'm sure you can
guess what they
were for.

13

I had to leave the sundews when the clouds rolled in. But as soon as I got home, I sent off for some sundew seeds of my own.

The seeds weren't just for ordinary sundews, though. They were for Giant African sundews. I sowed them in a pot of moss and covered it with glass. I watered the pot every day, with rainwater straight from the water barrel.

Soon the seeds started to sprout and I had dozens of baby sundews. They grew and grew, until they were nearly big enough to start catching things.

Then one day I watered them with the wrong sort of water — and every single one died.

I gave up on sundews after that,
but I did grow a Venus flytrap.
It lived on the windowsill and
caught insects. Each of its leaves
had a hinge down the middle,
several little trigger hairs, and a
spiky rim.

When a fly or a wasp walked
over a leaf, it was perfectly safe
if it didn't touch any of the hairs.
It was even safe if it touched
just one of the hairs. But if it
touched two of the hairs,
then …

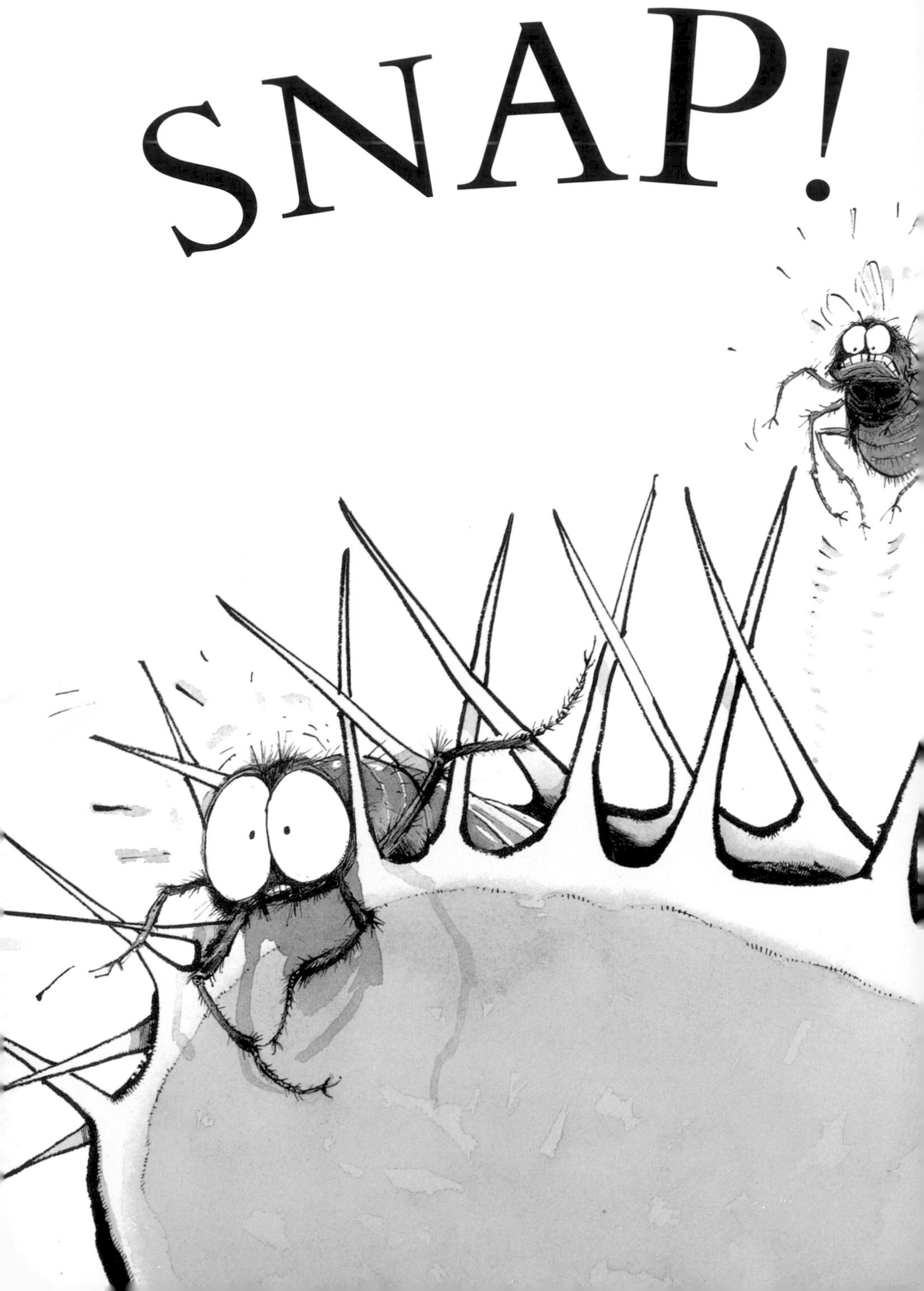
SNAP!

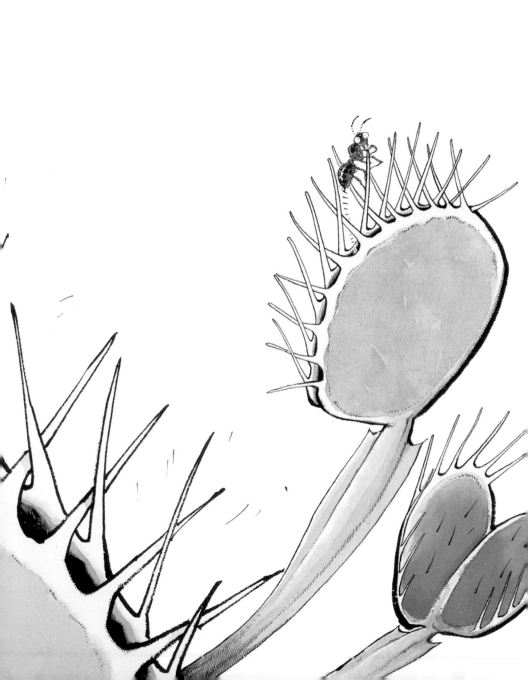

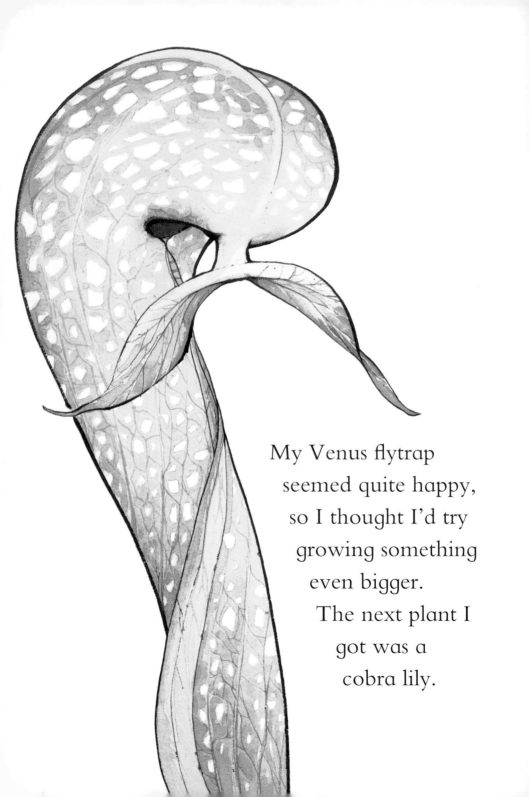

My Venus flytrap
seemed quite happy,
so I thought I'd try
growing something
even bigger.
The next plant I
got was a
cobra lily.

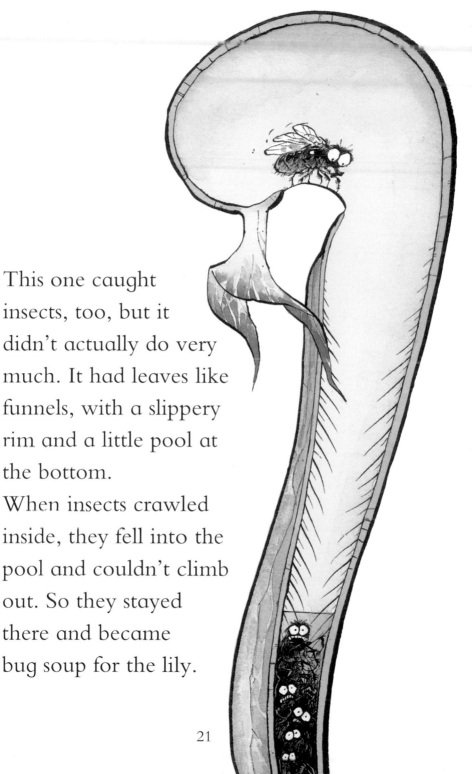

This one caught insects, too, but it didn't actually do very much. It had leaves like funnels, with a slippery rim and a little pool at the bottom.

When insects crawled inside, they fell into the pool and couldn't climb out. So they stayed there and became bug soup for the lily.

I was quite happy with my cobra lily.
Surely it was the biggest carnivorous
plant of all. But then my friend told
me about pitcher plants.

Pitchers are even bigger, she said,
but they are very difficult to grow.
In that case, I thought, I'll just go
and find some wild ones.

So I went –
all the way to Malaysia.

And there, growing up the trees at the edge of the jungle, were hundreds of pitcher plants. Fat red ones, thin yellow ones, curly green ones, all waiting for flies.

I didn't see the biggest
pitcher plant of all, though.
It's called the Rajah pitcher
plant and it grows on Kinabala,
which is 4,000 metres high.
It's the tallest mountain in Borneo.
It has pitchers the size of footballs.
People say it can even catch some
kinds of squirrel, but I'm not
convinced.

One day I'll go and see for myself…

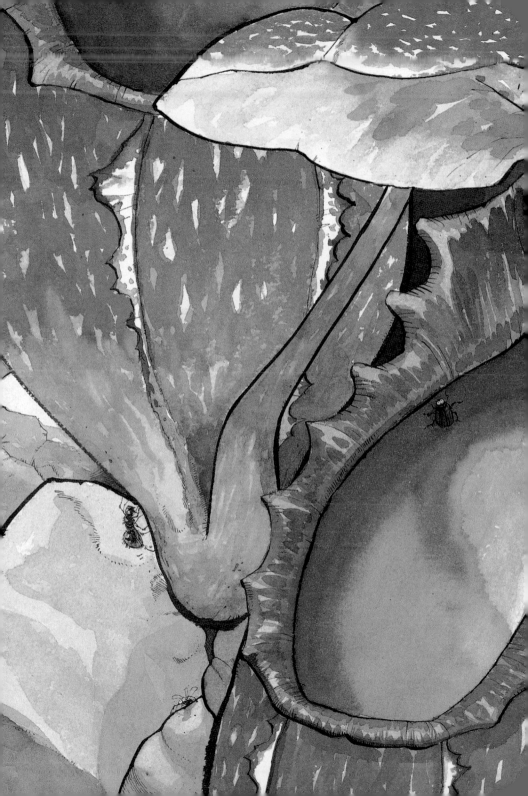

More about fly traps

There are hundreds of different kinds of carnivorous plants and they grow all around the world.

Cobra lilies get their name because their leaves look like cobras, not because they eat them! Cobra lilies come from North America. Their leaves can grow to be 45 centimetres high.

There are over 200 different kinds of bladderwort. Most of them grow in ponds and rivers. They are usually quite small, with narrow leaves and stems.

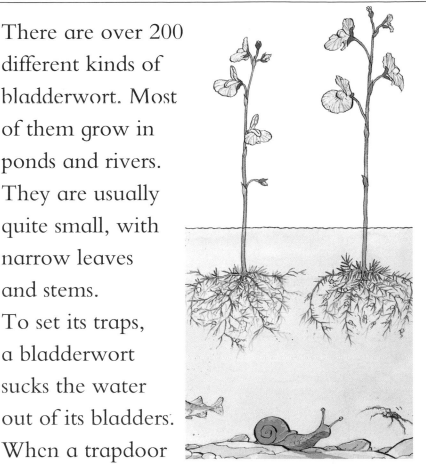

To set its traps, a bladderwort sucks the water out of its bladders. When a trapdoor opens, water rushes in, dragging the bug in with it. The bladderwort oozes special chemicals into the bladder. These dissolve the bug and the plant sucks it up.

There are over 80 sorts of sundew and they are found all over the world. Giant African sundews are the biggest. Their leaves can grow to be 45 centimetres long.

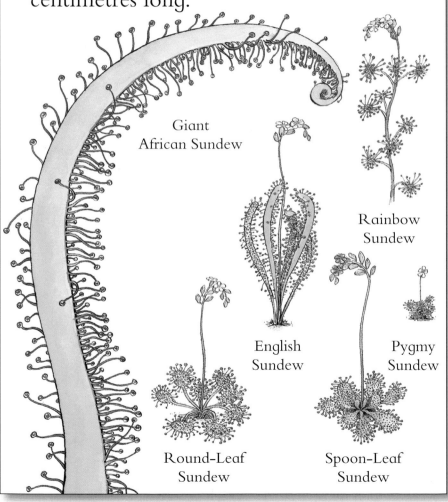

Giant African Sundew

Rainbow Sundew

English Sundew

Pygmy Sundew

Round-Leaf Sundew

Spoon-Leaf Sundew

When a bug gets stuck on a sundew, the leaf curls up slowly around it. Then the soft bits of the bug are

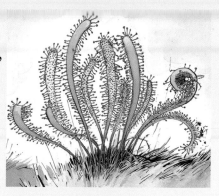

dissolved by chemicals and eaten. Afterwards, the leaf opens up again and the leftover bug bits fall off.

Butterworts are animal-eating plants, too, and often grow in the same places as sundews. They have sticky, flat leaves like flypaper. Little bugs stick to the leaves and slowly dissolve.

Venus flytraps only grow in one small part of North America. They are rare now because people have drained many of the marshes where they once lived.

Small insects such as ants can escape from a Venus flytrap – they're not big enough to be worth eating. But flies and wasps are a different story. Once caught, the more they struggle the tighter the leaf presses together. When the leaf is fully closed, it begins to dissolve its victim.

Pitcher plants are found in tropical countries. Like most other carnivorous plants, they usually grow where there is hardly any soil or where the soil is very poor. The pitchers' leaves look like vases, and they catch insects in the same way that cobra lilies do. There are some sorts of spider, and even some small tree frogs, that are able to live inside the pitchers. They cling to the slippery sides and grab the insects that fall in.

Index

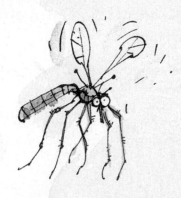

About the Author

Martin Jenkins is a conservation biologist. When not travelling to faraway jungles and mountain tops, he spends most of his time writing "serious things for the United Nations and various governments." *Fly Traps! Plants that Bite Back* is one of his first books for children.

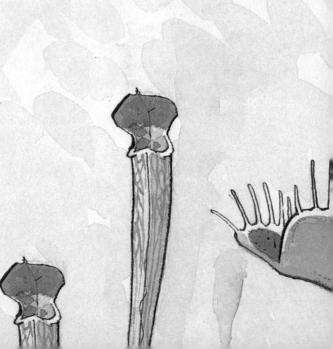

About the Illustrator

David Parkins recalls, "When I first
started out as an illustrator, I did a
book on wildlife and spent a year
tramping around fields drawing berries
and birds. So in a way, this book takes
me back to my roots, quite literally."

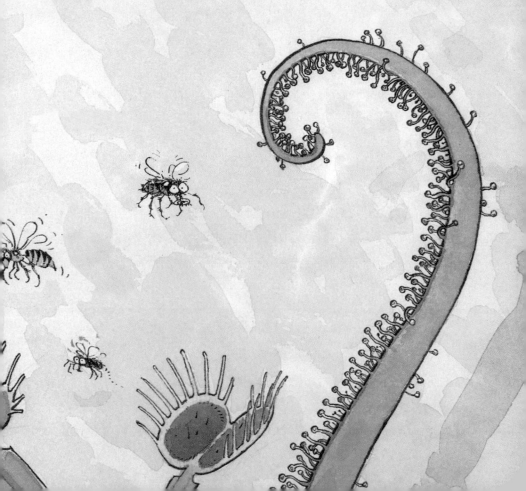

There are 10 titles in the
READ AND DISCOVER series.
Which ones have you read?

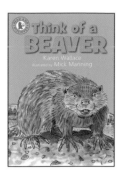

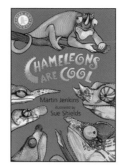

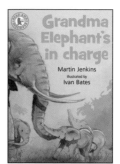

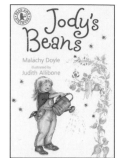

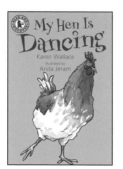

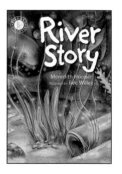

Available from all good booksellers